The Concise Illustrated Book of
Sharks

Rodney Steel

SMITHMARK

First published in the
United States of America by
GALLERY BOOKS
An imprint of W. H. Smith Publishers Inc.
112 Madison Avenue
New York, New York 10016

ISBN 0-8317-1689-4

Printed in Portugal

Front Cover: Mako Shark
Right: Oceanic WhiteTip
Back cover: Oceanic White Tip

Photographic Acknowledgements
Howard Hall 4, 8, 9, 13, 19, 20/21, 24, 27, 30, 31,
34, 37, 41, 45, 46; Living Ocean Society/Howard
Hall 29. Planet Earth Pictures 43; Alex Kerstitch/
Planet Earth Pictures 12; Ken Lucas/Planet Earth
Pictures 35.

All artworks by David Webb of Linden Artists.

CONTENTS

INTRODUCTION

Familiar to everyone, universally feared and admired, sharks nonetheless remain creatures of mystery. The most dangerous of all living sharks is the notorious great white, which may reach 9m (30 ft) in length, and yet no one knows how or where they reproduce, or how long they live. As recently as 1976, a totally unknown shark 4.5m (15 ft) long was found in the Pacific; dubbed the megamouth shark because of its cavernous mouth, it is scarcely conceivable that so large a fish could have escaped the notice of science for so long.

The oldest sharks so far discovered in the fossil record date back 350 million years, and before the end of the age of dinosaurs, 66 million years ago, modern sharks closely related to those in today's seas were already in existence. From the polar oceans to tropical seas, from abyssal depths to inland lakes, sharks have become the masters of their environment.

Some sharks are of such a large size and so highly specialized for the lethal business of killing that they are dangerous to humans, to the extent of being well-established man-eaters. Others, however, are harmless leviathans that simply subsist on the minuscule creatures forming the plankton which floats in the oceans like a living soup. A good many sharks are quite small, measuring only a few feet in length, and a few species are so diminutive that a fully grown specimen can be held in the palm of the hand.

It is sometimes claimed that sharks are primitive fish because their skeletons are basically made of cartilage – a tissue that does provide a convenient means of distinguishing sharks and similar cartilaginous forms (skates, rays, chimaeras), collectively known as chondrichthyans, from the bony fishes (such as herrings, salmon and other familiar types), which are classified as osteichthyans. Other significant differences between these two groups of fish are the absence in sharks of a cover (operculum) over the external gill openings, and the presence of dermal denticles covering the skin that have an internal structure incorporating a pulp cavity. Most sharks have five pairs of gills (some, six or seven); there are paired anterior (pectoral) and posterior (pelvic) fins to provide propulsion and steering, aided by a caudal (tail) fin which has an upper lobe supported by a continuation of the spine (angled upwards to a greater or lesser degree) and usually a fleshy lower lobe. One or two dorsal fins occur on the back, and most species also have a ventral anal fin just in front of the tail.

Predatory species have a pointed snout, and a pair of nostrils that are often connected to the mouth by furrows. The sense of smell is well developed and sight usually keen, while lateral line organs and pit organs on the body respond sensitively to the movement of water as the shark swims, and sensory pores on the head are apparently electro-receptors. Sharks can detect blood in the water from a substantial distance, are probably able to sense the electrical fields of living organisms, and can even 'hear' the low-frequency sounds generated by struggling, injured fish. The shark brain is quite complex for a fish, and their behaviour patterns refute suggestions that they are merely mindless killing automatons.

The apparently primitive frilled shark, the similarly conservative bullhead sharks (e.g. the Port Jackson shark), and the enigmatic six- and seven-gilled sharks are placed in three separate orders, probably representing survivors of archaic stocks. The majority of living sharks, including most of the really big ones, are classed together as the lamniforms (isurids like the great white and mako, carcharhinids such as the oceanic white tip, hammerheads, threshers, the whale shark, the megamouth shark, the basking shark, nurse sharks, sand sharks, smooth dogfish, spotted dogfish, swell sharks, and zebra sharks), while the squaliforms constitute a second assemblage of mainly rather small sharks (including dwarf species, as well as the bramble sharks, green dogfish, the humantin, the luminous shark, the Portuguese shark, and spiny dogfish) but with the quite large Greenland shark numbered among them. The angel fish and the saw sharks are usually referred to separate orders of their own, since they differ so radically from typical sharks.

ATLANTIC PORBEAGLE

Classification: *Lamna nasus* (family Isuridae); also known as mackerel shark, herring shark

Range: Boreal and warm temperate waters of the North Atlantic from the Barents Sea to South Carolina in the west and Madeira in the east, coming inshore during the summer months. Also possibly present in the southern hemisphere from southern Brazil and Argentina to South Africa, southern Australia, New Zealand and Chile

Coloration: Bluish-grey above, fading to white below, with a white patch at the posterior base of the first dorsal fin

Size: Up to about 3.5m (11 ft 6 in) in length

Description: Relatively common sharks in temperate seas, that feed voraciously on fish (notably herring, cod, whiting, hake, mackerel and dogfish), as well as squid and cuttlefish; they will on occasion attack man, and must be regarded as dangerous. The snout is pointed and overhangs a large crescentic mouth with prominent, slender smooth-edged teeth each of which has two accessory points (one either side of the main cusp). The first dorsal fin is large and located further forward than it is in the closely related mako sharks, while the crescentic tail has an additional subsidiary stabilizing keel each side beneath the main keel. The second dorsal fin and the anal fin are diminutive, and the pelvic fins small. Reproduction is ovoviviparous, but only two embryos from each oviduct normally develop, these four having eaten any unfertilised eggs while inside the mother; on emergence they are unusually large, weighing as much as 9kg (20 lb). On fine days porbeagles are frequently seen near the surface, swimming with the dorsal fin exposed. They provide indifferent sport, proving sluggish when hooked and never jumping. Additional species of porbeagle occur in the Pacific.

ANGEL FISH

Classification: *Squatina squatina* (family Squatinidae); also known as the monk fish, the common names being a reference to the shape of the pectoral fins, which are greatly expanded and extend forward to an angular 'shoulder' in fancied resemblance to an angel's wings or a monk's cowl. Alternatively, the name fiddle fish (because the shape resembles a musical instrument) is sometimes employed

Range: Eastern north Atlantic (southern Norway and the Shetlands to Morocco and the Canary Islands) and the Mediterranean

Coloration: Yellowish to nearly black above (commonly grey or brown), with darker spots or blotches and occasionally white lines or spots on the back; the undersides are white

Size: Up to 2.4m (8 ft) in length, and a weight of 77kg (170 lb)

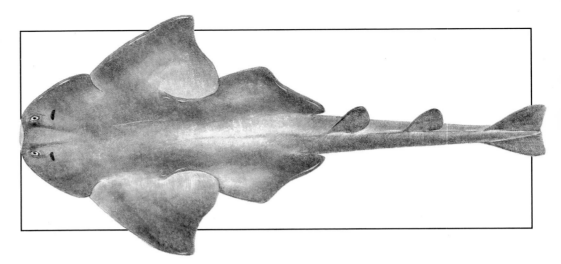

Description: With greatly flattened body and expanded pectoral fins, angel fish look superficially like skates or rays, but because they have gill openings extending onto the sides of the body from the ventral surfaces and pectoral fins, that are not attached to the sides of the head despite their forward projection, these odd-looking creatures are usually regarded as very specialized sharks. The pelvic fins are also very broad and wing–like, there are two spineless dorsal fins, an anal fin is absent, and the tail fin has its lower lobe larger than its upper lobe. A short and very broad snout has nostrils near its tip, and the eyes are in the upper side of the head, with large spiracles immediately behind them. Reproduction is ovo-viviparous, the 9-20 embryos per litter each being provided with a yolk sac. A bottom dweller preying on fish, crustaceans and molluscs, the angel fish is apparently territorial with a home area of about 150ha (375 acres), largely nocturnal, and prefers depths of 27-100m (about 90-325 ft). Other species occur in the western Atlantic and the Pacific, and a fossil representative of the family existed 140 million years ago.

BASKING SHARK

Classification: *Cetorhinus maximus* (family Cetorhinidae); also known in Wales and western Ireland as the sun fish

Range: Worldwide in temperate waters, from Newfoundland to Florida, southern Brazil to Argentina, Iceland and the Barents Sea to the Mediterranean and Senegal, Japan to China, Alaska to the Gulf of California, Ecuador to Peru, and southern Australia and New Zealand

Coloration: Bluish-grey, greyish-brown or sometimes nearly black with pale undersurfaces

Size: Up to about 9m (30 ft) in length, weighing 4 tonnes or more

Description: A huge but harmless denizen of nutrient-rich cool temperate seas. To feed, it ingests up to 9,000 litres (2,000 gallons) of sea water an hour through its vast mouth into the expanded gill and pharyngeal region, straining it through more than 1,000 rakers, each measuring about 10cm (4 in) in length, that are located along the hoop-like gill arches to extract planktonic food. Sometimes solitary, but often occuring in twos and threes, or even in groups of 60-100, this usually sluggish creature is capable of swimming with surprising speed when alarmed, the firm muscles, stiff fins and lunate tail fin with lateral stabilizing keels all being adaptations for powerful swimming. The skeleton is extensively calcified, and a huge oil-rich liver provides buoyancy (as well as generating a commercial demand for the species). Reproduction is presumably ovo-viviparous, females producing about 6 million tiny eggs from each ovary; the oviducts are richly endowed with small tag-like projections for nourishing developing embryos. Immature individuals up to 4.5m (15 ft) in length exhibit a thick, fleshy, hooked snout.

BLACK-MOUTHED DOGFISH

Classification: *Galeus melastomus* (family Scyliorhinidae); also known as the blackmouth catshark

Range: Eastern north Atlantic, from the Faeroe islands and Norway (Trondheim) south to Senegal and the Mediterranean

Coloration: Light grey or brownish, with a distinctive patterning of dark saddle blotches and spots; rear edges of dorsal fins and tail tip white.

Size: Up to 90cm (3 ft) in length

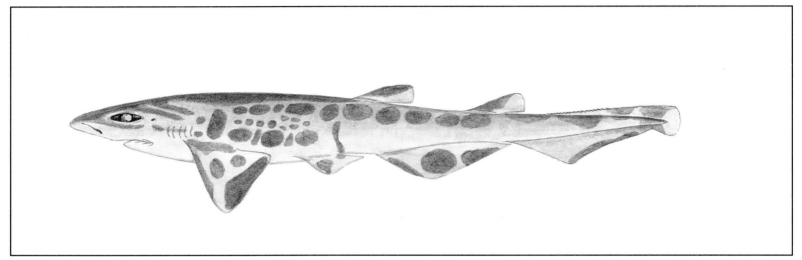

Description: As its common name implies, this species is remarkable for the unusual dark coloration of its large but rather short and very broadly arched mouth. The snout is flattened, although appearing pointed from the side, the two dorsal fins are quite small, and the tail almost straight with a moderately developed lower lobe. The pectoral fins are proportionately large and of substantial relative width, but the pelvic fins are small; the anal fin, in contrast, is well developed with a long base. The black-mouthed dogfish is a common deep water bottom-dweller occurring on the outer continental shelves, usually at 200–500m (650–1,625 ft), but sometimes encountered in shallower water and also recorded at depths as great as 1,000m (3,250 ft). Its food is principally invertebrate, especially shrimps and cephalopods, but it will also catch small bony fish (such as lanternfish) and small sharks. Reproduction is oviparous, with about 13 eggs forming a clutch, each egg case measuring about 3 by 6cm (1 1/4 by 2 1/4 in). The species is of limited commercial importance, but the flesh is sold fresh or salted for human consumption, and the skin makes a marketable leather.

Classification: *Echinorhinus brucus* (family Echinorhinidae); also known as the spinous shark or alligator shark
Range: Eastern Atlantic (North Sea to West Africa, and occasionally South Africa), Pacific (California, Hawaiian islands, Japan, Australasia), Mediterranean, and Indian Ocean (India and probably Oman); reported as a rare visitor from the western Atlantic (Massachusetts, Virginia, Argentina)

Coloration: Ash grey or dark brown above, occasionally with darker spots or white mottling, becoming paler or whitish ventrally
Size: Up to 3m (about 10 feet) in length

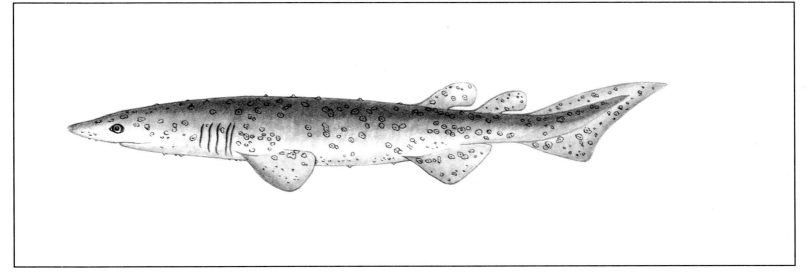

Description: A slender-bodied species whose skin incorporates button-like denticles scattered singly or in groups, some of which are surmounted by a tuft of small prickles resembling those on a bramble (hence the common name). Apparently a deep water bottom-dweller, occurring mostly at between 400 and 900m (1,300 and 2,925 ft), the bramble shark preys mostly on small fish (including spiny dogfish, ling, catfish, lizardfish) and crustaceans. The species has spineless dorsal fins set close together towards the tail, no anal fin and a caudal fin incorporating an upwardly directed axis with a well-developed lower lobe. The lips around the crescentic mouth are smooth, while the teeth each have 3–7 cusps, the middle point being strongly developed and outwardly directed. Reproduction is ovo-viviparous with 15-24 young in a litter. A separate species *(Echinorhinus cookei)* from the Pacific grows to nearly 4m (13 ft) in length. Fossil remains indicate that bramble sharks have been in existence for at least 50 million years.

BULL SHARK

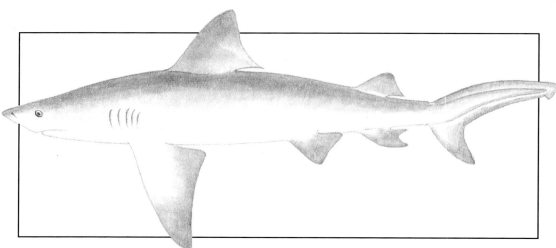

Classification: *Carcharhinus leucas* (family Carcharhinidae); also known as the cub shark, Zambezi shark, Ganges shark, and ground shark

Range: Worldwide in tropical, subtropical and temperate seas, except for the Mediterranean, frequenting inshore waters, river systems and associated lakes

Coloration: Pale or dark grey above, fading to white ventrally; fins with dusky-hued tips

Size: Up to 3.24m (about 10 ft 6 in) in length

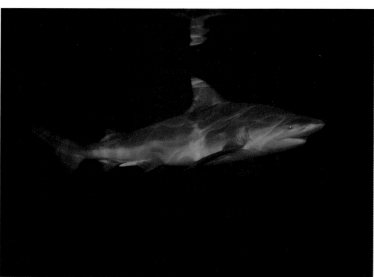

Description: This heavily built, broad-headed shark with a short, blunt snout is a confirmed man-eater, enjoying ample opportunities to take human victims along shore lines and in river systems. Bull sharks are evidently able to adapt their physiology to either freshwater or a marine environment, retaining less urea in their blood when they leave the sea and reducing the level of salts in their body fluids. They ascend rivers in Africa (e.g. the Zambezi), Australia, Iraq (the Tigris), India (the Ganges), North America (the Atchafalaya in Louisiana, the Mississippi in Illinois), and South America (the Peruvian Amazon), and occur in Lake Nicaragua, Lake Jamoer (New Guinea), Lake Izabal (Guatemala), the Panama canal, etc. The diet is basically fish (including other sharks, devil rays, sting rays, mackerel) and crabs. Reproduction is viviparous, gestation requiring nearly a year, with up to 12 embryos per litter. One known bull shark nursery area is to be found in the northern Gulf of Mexico, where shallow, brackish water bays and estuaries provide an ideal sanctuary for juveniles to reach a size at which they can take care of themselves in the open sea. *See also* Oceanic white tip shark, Silky shark.

CARPET SHARK

Classification: *Orectolobus maculatus* (family Orectolobidae); also known as the wobbegong (Australian aboriginal)
Range: Western Pacific, including Japan, the South China Sea, and the coasts of Australia
Coloration: Yellowish, greyish or brownish ground colour, with marbled, spotted, barred and striped markings
Size: Up to about 3m (10 ft) in length

Description: Carpet sharks spend most of their time lying partially buried in sand or mud waiting to engulf passing fish or crustaceans. Opening their jaws to create a suction effect, they draw victims inexorably into their mouths. The immobile habits of these sharks are reflected by their appearance – a flattened body, broad depressed head, and blunt snout. Tassels of skin line the sides of the head and sometimes also the chin, while the wide and almost straight mouth is furnished with a formidable dentition comprising slender single-pointed anterior teeth and multi-cusped lateral teeth. The anal fin extends back to the long straight caudal fin, and there are two dorsal fins, situated towards the tail. The external gill slits are large, with the last three or four on each side located above the base of the broad pectoral fins, and there is a large oblique, slit-like spiracle just below and behind the small eye. Reproduction is ovo-viviparous, with about 37 young in a litter. Carpet sharks are unaggressive, but because they like to lie concealed on the bottom in the shallows they are sometimes inadvertently trodden on by bathers, who in consequence get severely bitten. Several other species of *Orectolobus* occur around Australia, as well as one in Japanese and Chinese waters.

COMMON SAND SHARK

Classification: *Odontaspis taurus* (family Odontaspidae, the slender-toothed sharks, so named because of their large, smooth-edged awl-like teeth); also known as the sand tiger and the grey nurse

Range: Atlantic (Gulf of Maine to Bermuda, Southern Brazil to Argentina, Mediterranean to Cameroon), and Pacific Oceans (Japan to Indo-China, Australia), possibly peninsular India and Indonesia

Coloration: Yellowish-grey above, paler below; juveniles are spotted or blotched with brown or black

Size: Up to 3.5m (11 ft 6 in) in length

Description: Voracious predators that apparently sometimes co-operate in schools to attack shoals of fish; up to 45kg (100 lb) of fish have been found in the stomach of a single sand shark. The snout is short but sharply pointed, with a crescentic mouth and jaws that can be protruded to only a limited extent (in predatory sharks of the lamnid group like the great white the jaws can be protruded below the snout to augment the scope of the gape). Common sand sharks have a flattened head and elongate body, the two dorsal fins, the paired (pectoral and pelvic) fins and the anal fin all being of similar size; there is a distinct lower lobe to the tail fin. Prey includes cephalopods, lobsters and crabs in addition to fish. Only two young, about 1m (3 ft 3 in) long, are born in each litter, these two having allegedly consumed the other embryos within the mother's body. There is abundant evidence that they certainly eat eggs shed into the oviducts from the ovaries, embryos having been found with their bellies distended from ingested egg yolk. The common sand shark is a weak fighter if hooked and cannot be regarded as a game fish. Probably dangerous to man, the sand sharks of Australian waters have a particularly bad reputation. The species should possibly be regarded as a separate genus (*Eugomphodus*) to emphasize its distinction from the small-tooth sand shark (*Odontaspis ferox*).

CROCODILE SHARK

Classification: *Pseudocarcharias kamoharai* (family Pseudocarchariidae)
Range: Circum-tropical, abundant in some areas (e.g. the central Pacific), apparently rare elsewhere

Coloration: Dark brown, becoming whitish below, with a large white blotch between the angle of the mouth and the first gill slit; there is a narrow white margin to the dorsal and pectoral fins, and a narrow black margin to the lower and posterior margins of the tail fin

Size: The smallest known living member of the lamnid group, attaining a length of only about 110cm (about 3 ft 6 in)

Description: A small oceanic shark, usually found far out at sea but occasionally venturing inshore near the bottom, at depths down to 300m (975 ft). The eyes are disproportionately large, suggesting deep water or nocturnal habits, possibly rising towards the surface at night and descending away from the light by day. Elongation of the body is quite pronounced, with small paired fins and dorsal fins and a diminutive anal fin, but a powerful tail. The gill slits are unusually long, and the jaws possess exceptional protrusibility for feeding, although the feeding habits are not really known: the stomachs of crocodile sharks have been found to contain fish (especially luminous deep-sea bristlemouths), squid and shrimps, and the recurved awl-like front teeth supplemented by blade-like lateral teeth suggest a diet of active prey. Reproduction is ovoviviparous, with only two young surviving in each uterus, these juveniles apparently eating their prospective siblings while still inside the mother (up to nine fertilized eggs form in each oviduct). The crocodile shark is too small to constitute a real hazard to people, although it can snap viciously. The large and very oily liver, which

DWARF SHARK

Classification: *Squaliolus laticaudus* (family Scymnorhinidae); also known as the midwater shark

Range: Western Pacific (reported from Batangas Bay, Luzon, in the Philippines, and Suruga Bay, south-central Honshu, Japan)

Coloration: Jet black, with white fins
Size: No larger than 15cm (6 in) in length

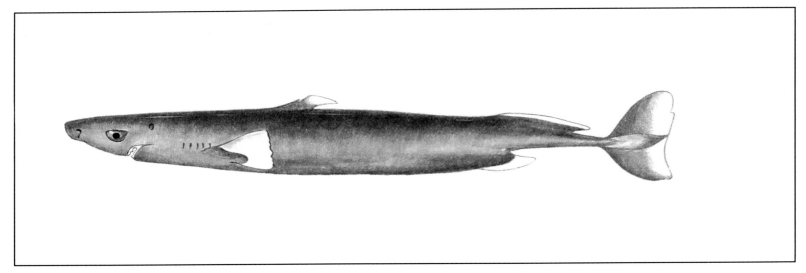

Description: The smallest known living shark, first reported from two specimens caught at 170 fathoms (about 300m) in the Philippines before World War I; five further specimens were caught nearly half a century later (in 1961) off Honshu, Japan. A cigar-shaped little fish, with a head making up about a third of its diminutive length, the dwarf shark has a pointed nose, thick fleshy lips, and a short broad tail incorporating an upwardly curved axis; there is no anal fin, but two dorsal fins are present, the first of which has a short spine in front of it (*Squaliolus* is the only shark of the scymnorhinid family to have such a spine) while the second has a long base and is situated well back towards the tail. The dentition is smooth-edged, upper teeth being slender, symmetrical and slightly recurved, while the lower series have each cusp directed obliquely outward. The dermal denticles are closely spaced and of varying size, their concave crowns giving a pebbled texture to the skin. Virtually nothing is known of how the dwarf shark lives. A second species (*Squaliolus sarmenti*) is blackish-brown in colour and 250mm (10 in) long: specimens have been taken at 800 fathoms (about 1,600m) off Madeira and (somewhat surprisingly) among shallow-water eel grass in the Bay of Biscay.

Classification: *Chlamydoselachus anguineus* (family Chlamydoselachiidae).

Range: A rare species from the eastern Atlantic (Norway to the Namibian coast, including the shores of Ireland, Scotland, Madeira and North Africa) and the Pacific (California, Japan, New Zealand, New South Wales). Apparently a denizen of deep cold waters of the continental shelves below 180m (about 550 ft)

Coloration: Dark brownish grey above, pale hued ventrally

Size: Up to 2m (6 ft 6 in) in length

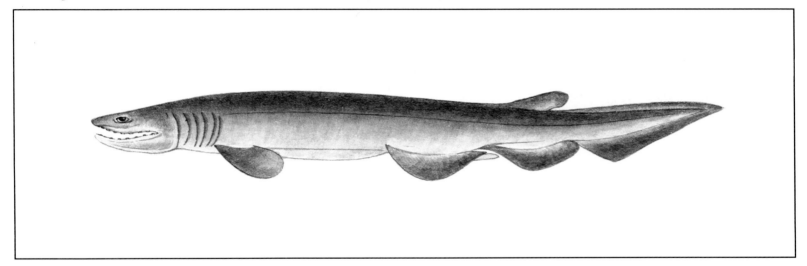

Description: A primitive shark of elongate shape with a flattened head and broad, rounded pectoral fins. The tail fin has a long, pointed upper lobe but almost no lower lobe, the single dorsal fin being located immediately above the anal fin. The pelvics are also posteriorly located, this concentration of dorsal, anal and pelvic fins in juxtaposition to the tail possibly affording a posterior fulcrum from which this spindle-shaped shark can strike its prey (which is unknown) from among rocks. The eyes are large and elongate, and a sliding jaw articulation enables the mouth to be gaped widely open. Tri-cuspid teeth are arranged in 14 rows across the upper and lower jaws, a total of about 300 individual teeth being present. The backbone displays hardly any calcification (it is formed principally by a primitively constructed notochord) and the six pairs of gills are each bordered by a broad frill of skin, which in the case of the first gill slit meets below the neck to suggest the common name of this shark. Reproduction is ovo-viviparous, with from 3 to 12 eggs hatching inside the female's body after a gestation period of up to two years.

17

GOBLIN SHARK

Classification: *Scapanorhynchus owstoni* (family Odontaspidae); also known as the elfin shark, and sometimes referred to a separate family of its own

Range: Western Indian Ocean, Atlantic and Pacific (Australia and Japan), occurring on the outer continental shelves down to about 550 fathoms (about 1,000m)

Coloration: Pinkish-white to greyish-brown, with paler underparts; fins exhibiting dark edges
Size: Up to 4.25m (about 14 ft)

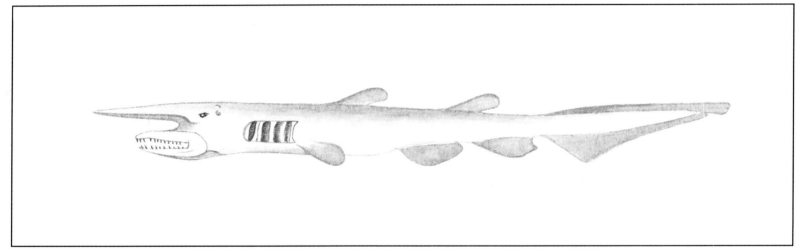

Description: A bizarrely long-snouted species, with jaws capable of protrusion to a remarkable degree. Frequenting deep water, it is probably a sluggish bottom feeder, but its life habits are virtually unknown. The two dorsal fins are smaller than the pelvic fins or the anal fin, and the lower lobe of the tail is poorly developed. Its teeth are smooth-edged and thorn-like at the front, supported on broad, two-rooted bases; the back teeth are modified to form a crushing mechanism. The goblin shark was first known from its fossil teeth, found in 90-million-year-old rocks at Mount Lebanon, Syria, during the 1880s. Described as *Rhinognathus,* a name then found to have already been used for a beetle, it was re-identified as *Scapanorhynchus,* but still remained just an obscure fossil. A few years later, the first example of a living goblin shark was caught in deep water off Yokohama, and the specimen was given the name of *Mitsukurina owstoni,* after Allen Owston (a foreign resident of Yokohama) and Professor Kakichi Mitsukuri, who were jointly responsible for its discovery. However, the living species and the numerous fossil forms of goblin shark all probably belong to the same genus.

GREAT BLUE SHARK

Classification: *Prionace glauca* (family Carcharhinidae); also known as the blue whaler

Range: Worldwide in tropical and warm temperate seas, small individuals occuring as far north as the British Isles and Alaska, as far south as Peru and New Zealand. One of the most widely distributed of all sharks

Coloration: Dark indigo blue above, shading to bright blue and finally white on the undersides

Size: Up to 4.5m (about 15 ft) in length

Description: One of the most elegantly proportioned and beautifully coloured of all sharks, the slender, long-snouted blue shark with elongate sickle-shaped pectoral fins and white-rimmed eyes occurs both in coastal waters and in the open ocean. They are often seen at the surface, swimming lazily with the first dorsal and the tip of the caudal out of the water, and probably never descend to great depths. Sluggish if undisturbed, they are powerful swimmers when seeking prey (e.g. herring, mackerel, sardines in European waters, spiny dogfish, cod, haddock, American pollock, anchovies, flying fish in the tropics) and it has been estimated they reach 64km/h (40 mph) during a short high-speed dash. Mating occurs in summer, the sperm being stored in the female until the following spring when ovulation occurs and fertilization is effected. Only the right uterus is present, in which 100 or more embryos spend up to a year developing, each attached to the uterine wall by a yolk-sac placenta; birth apparently occurs out at sea rather than inshore. The flesh of this species has an unattractive taste, and the great blue shark is of little commercial value.

GREAT WHITE SHARK

Classification: *Carcharodon carcharias* (family Isuridae); also known as the white pointer

Range: Worldwide in temperate and sub-tropical seas, preferring coastal areas (including shallow bays) but also encountered in the open ocean, especially near isolated oceanic islands. The range extends from Newfoundland to Florida, Brazil to Argentina, France to South Africa, Siberia to the Philippines, Australia and New Zealand, the Gulf of Alaska to the Gulf of California, and Panama to Chile

Coloration: Bluish-grey or slate-grey above (brownish in juveniles), shading to white on the belly, with the back edges of the fins darker hued

Size: Up to 9 m (30 ft) in length (females are slightly larger than males). A well nourished 6m (20 ft) specimen will weigh over 3,175kg (7,000 lb)

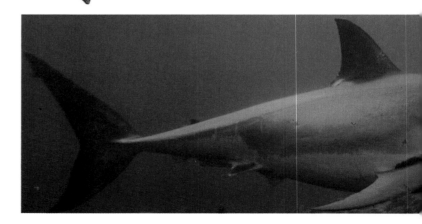

Description: The most notoriously dangerous man-eating shark, with a long record of fatal attacks on people. A massive creature, with a conical nose, triangular serrated teeth up to 7.5cm (3 in) long, very small second dorsal and anal fins, reduced pelvic fins, and prominent stabilizing keels either side of the crescentic tail. The eye is large with a deep black iris. A great white's diet includes fish, squid, and sea mammals (notably seals and sea lions, and whale carcases when whaling was widely practised). In the stomachs of great whites have been found whole sea lions, entire sharks, and occasionally human victims, but this fearsome species apparently often simply tears a mouthful of flesh from its prey and then swims away. A 6m (20 ft) great white can inflict a wound measuring a foot across with a single bite, exerting a force of 1.4kg/cm² (20 lb/sq in) with its jaws, so that victims normally die quickly from loss of blood. The breeding habits of the great white are virtually unknown, although it has been claimed that up to nine embryos 20–60cm (8–24 in) long have been found in a pregnant female. Extinct close relatives of the great white had teeth nearly twice the size of the living form and may have been 15m (50 ft) in length.

GREEN DOGFISH

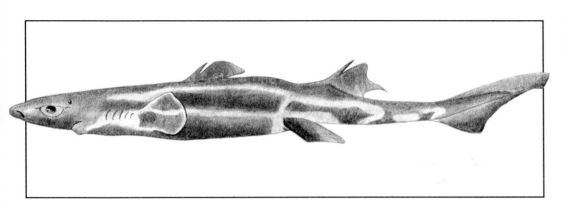

Classification: *Etmopterus virens* (family Squalidae)
Range: Northern Gulf of Mexico
Coloration: Dark brown or grey-black with a broad elongate black mark above and behind the pelvic fins and other black markings at the base of the tail and along its sides; the belly is black, shining an iridescent green in life
Size: Up to 30cm (1 ft) in length

Description: A diminutive slender-bodied shark normally found in schools at depths of 350-400m (1,140-1,300 ft), but sometimes descending as deep as 2,000m (about 7,000 ft). The two dorsal fins each have a spine at the front edge, the second dorsal being larger than the first. There is no anal fin, and the pelvic fins are of similar size to the pectorals. An elaborate system of luminous photophores (light organs) along the flanks and belly probably help individuals to maintain contact with other members of the school. The teeth of the upper and lower jaws are of different types, multi-cusped above, but broad and single-cusped below and obliquely set to form a continuous cutting edge. Analysis of the stomach contents of hundreds of captured specimens showed that a large part of their diet is composed on squid and octopus – cephalopods probably too large to be overcome by green dogfish unless these small but voracious sharks attack in packs. The ingested beaks and eyes are so large that the jaws and gullet must require considerable distension to swallow them. Reproduction is ovo-viviparous. Maintaining examples of this species in captivity has not proved to be a practicable proposition.

GREENLAND SHARK

Classification: *Somniosus microcephalus* (family Scymnorhinidae); also known as the sleeper shark or gurry shark

Range: Arctic and northern seas in water as cold as 0.6°C (about 34°F), ranging south to Japan, California, the Gulf of Maine and the Mediterranean

Coloration: Coffee brown to slaty grey or black above, with paler undersurfaces
Size: Up to 6m (about 20 ft) in length

Description: A stoutly proportioned shark with a small head, a bluntly rounded snout, no anal fin and a short, broad tail. The two dorsal fins are of similar size, and lack fin spines. Greenland sharks are massive bottom dwellers that subsist to a large extent on carrion (whale carcasses, offal from salmon canneries or seal-hunting centres), but also catch seals, porpoises, fish and crabs; their teeth are small, narrow and conical in the upper jaw, but markedly asymmetrical in the lower jaw, with unserrate outwardly directed cusps and notched outer edges. Small crustaceans parasitize the eyes of *Somniosus,* and it has been surmised that they act as a lure to fish upon which the shark preys. In spring young Greenland sharks come inshore, followed a little later by the adults, and they do not return to deep water until the autumn. Reproduction is ovoviviparous, with about ten embryos in a litter. Sleeper sharks occur in the southern Pacific *(Somniosus antarcticus),* and since they have been photographed 1,890m (6,200 ft) deep off Oahu it is possible that the northern and southern populations are really a single species that transits the equatorial latitudes in deep cold water. The liver is rich in oil and the skin is commercially valuable, but the flesh is toxic if eaten fresh (it can, however be eaten if salted or well boiled).

Classification: *Oxynotus centrina* (family Squalidae, but sometimes assigned to a separate family, the Oxynotidae); also known as the angular rough shark or prickly dogfish

Range: Eastern Atlantic (British Isles to Senegal and possibly South Africa) and the Mediterranean

Coloration: Brown, dark grey or reddish-brown
Size: Up to 1m (3 ft 3 in) in length

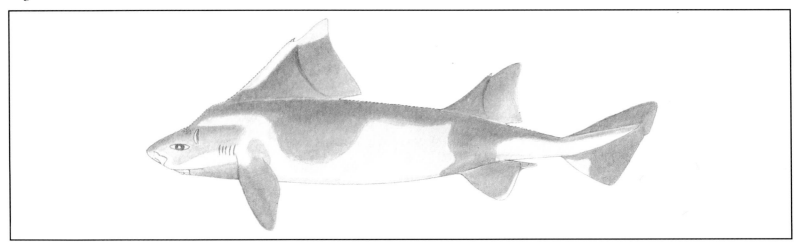

Description: A bottom-dwelling shark of markedly ungainly appearance with large prominent denticles that give it a very rough and prickly skin (hence the common names), which occurs at depths of 30-500m (100-1,625 ft) and feeds principally on hard-skinned prey. The robustly proportioned body is of triangular cross-section with a high back on which the two large dorsal fins are each preceded by a stout spine originating at about the mid-point of the fin base, projecting only very slightly from the front edge, and in the case of the first dorsal sometimes standing straight up or even inclining forwards. Longitudinal ridges occur low down on the flanks in front of the pelvic fins, and the tail is rather small. The upper teeth are arranged in a triangular patch on the roof of the mouth with two or three smooth-edged teeth in the first row and a greater number in each of the six or so succeeding series; the lower dentition comprises a single row of blade-like, backward-pointing, finely serrate teeth. Around the mouth there are thick, complexly folded spongy lips. Reproduction is ovo-viviparous, with up to about eight young in a litter. Rough sharks also occur in the western south Pacific.

LEMON SHARK

Classification: *Negaprion brevirostris* (family Carcharhinidae)

Range: Inshore waters of the western Atlantic and Caribbean, from New Jersey to southern Brazil; also present off the west African coast, and in the eastern Pacific (Gulf of California to Ecuador)

Coloration: Yellowish-brown, with a yellowish belly; juveniles are dark brown or darkish grey

Size: Up to about 3.5m (about 11 ft 6 in) in length

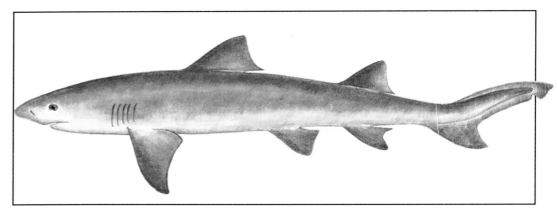

Description: A common inshore species, usually encountered at a depth of about 20 fathoms (36m), rarely occurring as deep as 50 fathoms (90m). It sometimes occurs offshore in surface waters, but the rather small eye is apparently not designed for vision in the poorly illuminated depths: ocular adaptation to bright light is rapid, but maximum dark adaptation requires over an hour. The snout is short and wide, with smooth-edged teeth erect in the front of the jaws but becoming oblique towards the corners of the mouth. The second dorsal fin is almost as large as the first, and considerably exceeds the anal fin in size. Mating occurs in spring and early summer, with gestation lasting about a year. Development is ovo-viviparous, 5-17 young (each about 60cm (2 ft) long) comprising a litter. Lemon sharks sometimes gather in loose schools of 20 or so individuals, often segregated by sex. Food includes fish (among them stingrays, which frequently leave their spines in the sharks' jaws) and octopus. The heavy hide makes an excellent leather, the large fins are valued by Chinese populations for soup, and the meat is of good quality. In addition, the liver is rich in vitamin A. Lemon sharks are very tolerant of high water temperatures (up to 29.5°C, 85°F), and restriction of movement when caught on set lines.

LESSER SPOTTED DOGFISH

Classification: *Scyliorhinus canicula* (family Scyliorhinidae); also known as the rough hound, small spotted dogfish, robin huss, suss, land dog, row hound, cur fish, kennett, daggar, morgay, daw fish

Range: Eastern North Atlantic (from Norway and the British Isles to Senegal) and Mediterranean

Coloration: Yellowish grey with dark blotches on the upper surfaces, becoming almost white ventrally

Size: Up to 1m (3 ft 3in) in length

Description: A commercially important food fish that lives on small fish and invertebrates (molluscs, worms, crustaceans) from the sea floor at depths of 20–400 fathoms (54–720m). Although there are two dorsal fins, they are situated well back towards the tail, even the first one (the larger) being above or even behind the pelvic fins. A narrow shelf overhangs the eyes to provide them with a measure of protection from injury. These small common sharks reproduce oviparously by laying eggs. During copulation the male wraps his tail laterally around the female to fertilize her eggs internally. Eventually, the female lays her eggs (one per oviduct at a time) in rectangular horny capsules measuring 4–6 by 10–12cm (1 1/2–2 1/2 by 4–4 3/4 in), swimming among seaweeds, gorgonians, sponges or other branched structures while laying so that the egg cases become attached to these projections by means of 1m (3 ft 3 in) long filaments that arise from each corner and spiral down to a length of only 15cm (6 in). Development requires 8–9 months, the embryo being attached to a large yolk sac but nonetheless making swimming movements that pump a flow of water through the permeable membrane of the transparent capsule to provide for respiration. When hatched, the young are about 10cm (4 in) long and bear dark diagonal stripes that eventually break up into spots.

LUMINOUS SHARK

Classification: *Isistius brasiliensis* (family Scymnorhinidae); also known as the cookie-cutter shark

Range: Subtropical and tropical waters of the Atlantic, Pacific, and southern Indian Ocean down to about 600m (2,000 ft)

Coloration: Greyish or brownish above, with a dark ring around the neck in the vicinity of the gill openings and white-tipped fins

Size: Up to 45cm (1 ft 6 in) in length

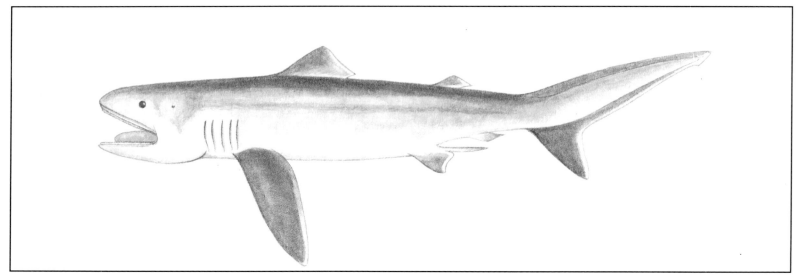

Description: A diminutive mid-water shark of elongate shape with pectoral and pelvic fins of modest proportions, no anal fin, and a short broad tail. The two small, closely adjacent dorsal fins lack spines and are situated near the tail. Bright luminescent organs occur along the belly and in diminishing numbers up the flanks, giving off a greenish glow. The name cookie-cutter shark aptly describes the teeth: the upper ones are unremarkable, being slender, thorn-like and widely spaced, but those in the lower series are large and triangular with a smooth or only partly serrate edge. When worn, a whole set is apparently replaced simultaneously. At the corners of the mouth there is a greatly expanded lip-fold supported by special cartilages, and it seems that *Isistius* attacks tuna, porpoises, whales, large sharks, and (especially) squid by using its sucker-like lips to secure a purchase and then removing a disc of meat with its extraordinary teeth. It is a very difficult shark to catch, because it can quickly bite its way out of a trawl net. Luminous sharks apparently congregate in schools, and probably reproduce ovo-viviparously.

MAKO SHARK

Classification: *Isurus oxyrinchus* (family Isuridae); also known as the sharp nosed mackerel shark and the blue pointer
Range: Worldwide in temperate and tropical seas, from the Gulf of Maine to northern Argentina, the British Isles to South Africa, Japan to New Zealand, and the Indian Ocean
Coloration: Dark grey or dark blue above, white underparts
Size: Up to 4m (about 13 ft) in length

Description: Open ocean sharks that customarily swim just below the surface showing only the tall first dorsal fin, which is located further back than in the similar (and closely related) porbeagle. The second dorsal is tiny, as is the anal fin, and the pectoral fins are much longer than the pelvics. Either side of the crescentic tail there is a prominent stabilizing keel. This slenderly proportioned species has acquired a famous reputation with big-game fishermen because of its propensity to jump energetically when hooked, sometimes leaping 4.5m (15 ft) clear of the water. It preys principally on fish, including swordfish, a 54.5kg (120 lb) example of which was found to have been swallowed whole, complete with sword, by a 330kg (730 lb) mako taken near Bimini, in the Bahamas; other fast-swimming fish regularly caught by makos include mackerel, tunny, herrings and tarpon, this shark's smooth-edged teeth being ideally suited to securing such agile prey. Reproduction is ovo-viviparous, apparently with pre-natal cannibalism. A separate species (*Isurus alatus*) possessing inordinately long pectoral fins is found in the tropical Indian, Pacific and Atlantic Oceans. Mako sharks are regarded as dangerous to man, and will frequently attack fishing boats, leaving their characteristic teeth embedded in the planking.

MEGAMOUTH SHARK

Classification: *Megachasma pelagios* (family Megachasmidae)
Range: Tropical Pacific Ocean
Coloration: Dark grey to blue-black dorsally, pale-toned flanks and grey undersides; lower surface of head and lower jaw grey mottled with black. White edges to the upper rear margins of the pectoral and pelvic fins, rear edges of anal, dorsal and caudal fins white
Size: Up to 4.5m (about 15 ft) in length

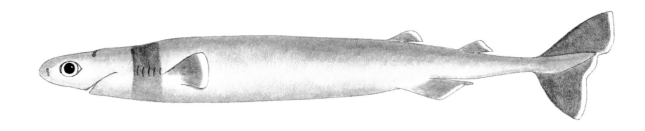

Description: Unknown to science until 1976, when a specimen was found entangled in the parachute anchor of a U.S. oceanographic research vessel off Oahu. With an enormously distensible mouth and pharynx, protrusible jaws containing over 100 rows of small hooked teeth, and gill rakers along the edges of the internal gill openings, the megamouth shark is evidently a plankton-eater, subsisting primarily on shrimps. The pelvic fins and the second dorsal are quite small, while the caudal fin has an elongate upper lobe. Weak swimming capability is indicated by its poorly calcified skeleton, soft loose skin, flabby connective tissue and muscles and very flexible fins; feeding is apparently accomplished by cruising through shoals of shrimps with the jaws protruded, occasionally closing the mouth and contracting the pharynx to expel the water and trap shrimps on the gill rakers. Several specimens of the megamouth shark have now been recovered, including a live example taken off California in 1990 and subsequently released. Nothing is known of the reproductive habits of this species. It is quite harmless to man.

Classification: *Ginglymostoma cirratum* (family Orectolobidae)
Range: Western Atlantic from Rhode Island to Brazil; eastern Atlantic, from the Cape Verde islands to Gabon; eastern Pacific from the Gulf of California to Peru
Coloration: Uniformly greyish- to yellowish-brown, with small scattered black spots on young individuals
Size: Up to 3.75m (12 ft)

Description: A sluggish, in-shore shark which spends most of its time on the bottom or resting in submarine caverns. It is largely a scavenger, but will also take small fish and invertebrates such as squid, cuttlefish, shrimps, lobsters, crabs, sea urchins, shellfish, etc. The head is short and blunt, with a snub nose and straight mouth, while the body is elongate and of circular cross-section, terminating in a long, upwardly angled tail; two dorsal fins are present, located well back towards the caudal region. The small eyes of the nurse shark suggest that it lacks the sharp vision of more actively hunting sharks, but there is a pair of prominent sensory nasal barbels and a conspicuous groove connects each nostril with the mouth – features indicative of bottom-dwelling habits, the sense of smell being well developed. Reproduction is ovo-viviparous, mature eggs being of very large size (100mm, 4 in, in length) with up to 28 young in a litter. If accidentally disturbed or deliberately teased it can bite severely enough to inflict a serious wound with its small but pointed teeth. Related species of *Ginglymostoma* live in the Pacific and Indian Oceans.

OCEANIC WHITE TIP

Classification: *Carcharhinus longimanus*, (family Carcharhinidae). This genus (see also Silky shark, Bull shark), includes some 25 species, most of which are coastal denizens of the tropics and subtropics, although *Carcharhinus* has been reported at latitudes as high as 40 degrees

Range: Worldwide in temperate offshore waters, with the possible exception of the Mediterranean, preferring sea temperatures of 10-30°C. (50-80°F) (optimum 20°C, 68°F)

Coloration: Varying from ochre to greyish brown above, with light hued ventral surfaces. The fin tips of adults are mottled white

Size: Length up to 3.6m (12 ft)

Description: A powerful member of the carcharhinid group readily identifiable by white mottling at the tips of its fins (in adults), the broadly rounded outline of the first dorsal fin, and the very long pectoral fins. Oceanic white tips are exceedingly abundant in the open ocean, hunting for fish in the surface waters of seas over 100 fathoms (180m) deep, and have acquired a reputation for tenacity and fearless aggression in their attacks, although tending to be rather slow moving. Since they rarely venture inshore, however, they pose only a limited danger to man. The snout is laterally flattened and broadly rounded in outline, with the nostrils located well forward. In the upper jaw the serrated teeth are triangular, while the lower series are more slender although rising from a broad base. Immature individuals often have black-tipped fins, but these become white mottled at maturity. Reproduction is viviparous, large females bearing up to 20 young.

Classification: *Heterodontus portusjacksoni* (family Heterodontidae); also known as the oyster crusher or pig shark. One of the bullhead sharks, which include species from Japan, China, Indonesia, western South America, California, western Mexico, Australia, South Africa, and the Galapagos Islands

Range: Temperate and subtropical Australian waters, including a reported occurrence in New Zealand and occurring down to nearly 100 fathoms (180m). Absent from the tropical coasts of the Northern Territory and Queensland

Colour: Buff, with scattered dark brown spots

Size: Up to 1.5m (5 ft) in length

Description: Inelegant predators of molluscs, fish, crustaceans and sea urchins that are harmless to man and flee to shallow water if approached. The head is short and blunt, with small sideways-looking eyes beneath elongate protective ridges and conspicuous grooves connecting the nostrils to the mouth, while the pectoral fins are large and the two dorsal fins each have a large blunt supporting spine. The tail is quite short, and the anal fin relatively small. Teeth at the front of the jaws are of only moderate size, but the back teeth form a crushing mechanism to break open shellfish and other hard prey. Bullhead sharks force their way beneath rocks to find shellfish and sea urchins, using the dorsal fin spines and the bony ridges above the eyes. As a result the dorsal fin spines are often considerably worn down. Females each lay 10-16 eggs in shallow water in the late winter and spring (July to October). The horny, dark brown egg cases, about 15cm (6 in) long, have two tough spiral flanges that enable them to be wedged among rocks.

PORTUGUESE SHARK

Classification: *Centroscymnus coelolepis* (family Squalidae); also known as the Portuguese dogfish
Range: Temperate waters of the eastern Atlantic (Iceland to Madeira and Sierra Leone, southern Africa), northern shores of the western Atlantic (Grand Banks to Delaware), the western Pacific (South China Sea, New Zealand), and the western Mediterranean
Coloration: Blackish brown
Size: Up to 115cm (nearly 4 ft) in length

Description: A stockily built shark with two small dorsal fins (each preceded by a diminutive spine), a very short snout, relatively large pectoral fins, a short broad tail, and no anal fin. The upper teeth are slender, the lower ones blade-like with short oblique cusps. Along the sides of the body the denticles are circular, very large and smoothly surfaced in mature individuals, giving this shark something of the scaly appearance typical of bony fishes. Although a common species with an extensive geographical range, the Portuguese shark is poorly known. It apparently lives near the bottom of the continental slopes, usually about 400m (1,300 ft) down, although it is known to descend as deep as 3,675m (nearly 12,000 ft): the preferred water temperature is 5-13°C (41-55°F). Reproduction is ovo-viviparous with 13-16 young in a litter, and the food principally bony fishes. The species has some commercial value, either for fishmeal or, when dried and salted, for human consumption. Other species of the genus *Centroscymnus* occur in the Pacific, Atlantic and Indian Oceans, while fossil specimens have been found in rocks laid down during the age of reptiles, over 65 million years ago.

Classification: *Pristiophorus schroederi* (family Pristiophoridae); also known as the Bahamas sawshark

Range: South-east coast of Florida to the Bahamas, at depths of 350-500 fathoms (630-900m), but sometimes encountered in shallow water

Coloration: Light greyish brown above, white below
Size: Up to about 1m (3 ft 3 in) in length
Description: *Pristiophorus* can be instantly recognized by its greatly elongate snout

armed with sharp tooth-like structures projecting sideways from each edge and the two long sensory barbels extending downwards halfway along. Superficially the sawsharks resemble the sawfish (which are rays), but in *Pristiophorus* the five pairs of gill slits are located along the sides of the neck region, not below it. The pectoral fins are broad and fan-shaped, the pelvic fins of only moderate size, and the tail almost straight with lateral keels and a quite well developed lower lobe. Two dorsal fins are present, but there is no anal fin. Sawsharks are bottom-dwellers, apparently making use of their long snouts to plough along the muddy sea floor, using the long barbels for detecting prey. The true teeth, inside the mouth, are small thorn-like single cusped structures, in several functional rows. Reproduction is ovo-viviparous, the 'teeth' of the saw being folded against the snout until the dozen or so juveniles emerge to avoid damage to the mother's birth canal. Other species of *Pristiophorus* occur in the Pacific, and a six-gilled sawshark (*Pliotrema*) is present off South Africa.

SCALLOPED HAMMERHEAD

Classification: *Sphyrna lewini* (family Sphyrnidae); also known (in Mexico) as the yellow hammerhead

Range: Warm temperate and tropical seas: the Mediterranean; the Atlantic from New Jersey to Brazil and from Senegal to Zaire; The Indian Ocean; the Red Sea; and the Pacific Ocean from Japan to Queensland and from southern California to Ecuador.

Coloration: Grey-brown above, becoming paler ventrally; dusky or black pectoral fin tips

Size: Up to 3.25m (about 10 ft 6 in)

Description: The hammerheads are distinguished by a bizarre specialization of the head, which is broadly expanded and greatly flattened, with the eyes and nostrils situated at its outer extremities. No proven explanation of this extraordinary structure has been put forward: it may be an aid to manoeuvrability (acting as a hydrofoil), or by widely separating the eyes and nostrils it could perhaps aid visual and olfactory acuity. The wide head is also unusually well supplied with electrically-sensitive receptors which probably pick up bio-electricity from stingrays (a favourite prey of hammerheads) lying half buried on the sea floor. The first dorsal fin is of narrow triangular shape and much larger than the small second dorsal, while the tail is relatively long, with a well developed lower lobe. The teeth are smooth-edged and backwardly inclined, well adapted for securing fish (other sharks, skates, stingrays, herring, mullet, mackerel etc) and invertebrates such as squid and shrimps. Reproduction is viviparous, with yolk-sac placentas tightly attaching the 30 or so embryos to the uterine wall. Some hammerhead species achieve 6m (20 ft) in length, others are small (up to just 1.5m, 5 ft, long) with only an incipiently broadened head.

SEVEN-GILL SHARK

Classification: *Heptranchias perlo* (family Hexanchidae), also known as the perlon
Range: Mediterranean Sea, Atlantic (North Carolina to the northern Gulf of Mexico, southern Brazil to Argentina, Morocco to Angola), Pacific (Japan and China, Indonesia and Australasia, northern Chile) and Indian Oceans
Coloration: Browny-grey, paler below
Size: About 1.4m (4 ft 6 in) in length

Description: The seven-gill like the six-gill shark, is a comb shark, with the comb-like lower teeth characteristic of this family. The head is narrow, terminating in a tapering snout, and there are, as the name implies, seven pairs of gills (two more than is customary in sharks). There is only a single dorsal fin, located almost above the anal fin, and as in all comb sharks the vertebrae are poorly calcified and the jaw articulation is of a relatively primitive type. The seven-gill is a deep-water bottom-dweller, living essentially on fish, and is not regarded as dangerous to man; it has occasionally been reported to enter shallow roadsteads or lagoons in tropical west Africa. Pregnant females have been found to contain up to 20 embryos, each with a large oval yolk sac, the length at birth being about 25cm (10 in). Seven-gill sharks distinguished by a broadly rounded snout and a disproportionately long tail are often regarded as belonging to a separate genus *(Notorynchus)*, but they may well be merely species of *Heptranchias*. These forms occur in the colder waters of the Pacific and the western South Atlantic, ranging up to 4m (13 ft) in length.

SHARP-NOSED SHARK

Classification: *Rhizoprionodon terraenovae* (family Carcharhinidae)
Range: North-eastern Atlantic, from the Bay of Fundy south to Yucatan

Coloration: Brownish to olive grey above, white below; the pectoral fins have white margins, the two dorsals are dusky tipped, and large individuals exhibit small light spots
Size: About 1m (3 ft 3 in) in length

Description: A moderate-sized shark with a notably pointed snout that is common on the continental shelves of eastern North America in warm-temperate and tropical waters, sometimes occuring as deep as 280m (about 900 ft) but usually a denizen of the shallows. It occasionally enters brackish estuaries and river mouths, but does not penetrate far into fresh water. The second dorsal fin is small and situated above the posterior half of the anal fin, very close to the tail, which has a long upper lobe. Sharp-nosed sharks have serrate teeth when they are adult that are directed obliquely backwards: the diet includes small bony fish such as menhaden, snake eels, silversides and wrasses, together with shrimps, crabs, worms and molluscs. Reproduction is viviparous with a yolk-sac placenta, up to seven young being born at a time after a gestation period of 10-11 months (in May-June in the Gulf of Mexico, June-August further north). The sharp-nosed shark is harmless to man.

Classification: *Carcharhinus falciformis* (family Carcharhinidae); also known as the grey reef shark or sickle shark
Range: Tropical and subtropical waters of the Atlantic (Massachusetts to southern Brazil, Madeira to northern Angola), the Pacific (Baja California to Peru, China to New Zealand) and the Indian Oceans
Coloration: Dark brown to dark grey above, white below; pectoral and pelvic fins dusky-tipped
Size: Up to 3.3m (nearly 11 ft) in length

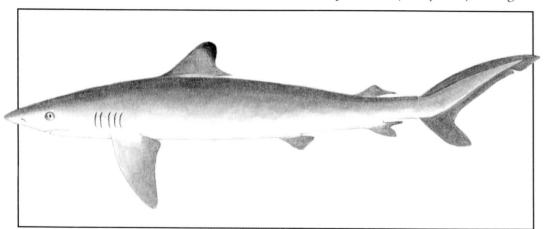

Description: The lithe, uniformly coloured 'requiem' sharks (so named because sailors believed they appeared in good weather) of the genus *Carcharhinus* are collectively referred to as 'whalers' on account of their predilection for the offal that was to be found floating near whaling stations. Very active at night, these sharks in fact live mostly on fish, which are sought in the upper layers of tropical and warm temperate seas (some species will also enter fresh water). Adults lack a spiracle, and the second dorsal fin is only slightly more than half the size of the first dorsal. The tail has a distinct lower lobe and an elongate upper lobe.

Carcharhinus falciformis owes its common name to the small flat dermal denticles of its skin, which give it a silky texture. If preparing to attack it displays agonistic behaviour — an erratic manner of swimming with the back arched, the snout raised, and the pectoral fins lowered. Because of its size and aggressive disposition, particularly if cornered, this shark should be regarded as potentially dangerous to man. Reproduction is viviparous, gestation requiring 10-11 months, with up to 14 embryos in a litter. See also bull shark, oceanic white tip shark.

SIX-GILL SHARK

Classification: *Hexanchus griseus* (family Hexanchidae), the blunt-nose six-gill
Range: Temperate waters of the Mediterranean and the Atlantic (North Carolina to Venezuela, southern Brazil to northern Argentina, Iceland to Nigeria, Angola to South Africa), Pacific (Aleutian Islands to Mexico, Chile) and Indian Oceans
Coloration: Uniform dark brownish grey above, shading to a paler tone below, with a slight coloured streak along the middle of each flank
Size: Up to 5m (16 ft 3 in) in length

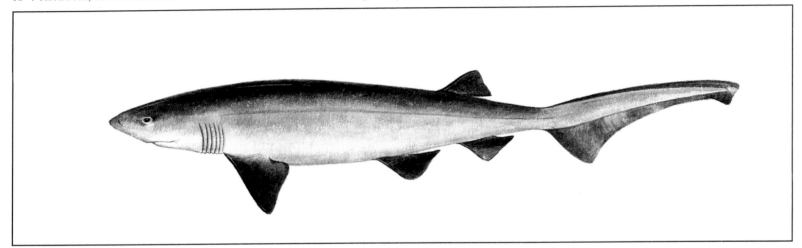

Description: The six-gill sharks or grisets are comb sharks (see also seven-gill shark), so named because their lower teeth bear an unmistakable similarity to a series of combs. The extra pair of gill slits (most sharks have only five pairs) is a noteworthy characteristic, as is the presence of only a single dorsal fin located well back towards the tail, poorly calcified vertebrae, and a primitive type of jaw articulation. The blunt-nose six-gill is a bottom-dwelling deep sea species that spends the day resting on the bottom and ascends at night to feed in the surface waters. It is known to dive as deep as 1,850m (5,900 ft), and if hooked will frequently simply dive deeper and deeper, so that unless the fisherman is operating from a very large boat it is necessary to cut the line. Reproduction is ovoviviparous, a female blunt-nose six-gill 4.5m (14 ft 6 in) long having been found to contain 108 embryos, and free-swimming mouse-grey coloured juveniles measuring 40–70cm (16–28 in) have been caught. A smaller species, *Hexanchus vitulus* (the big-eyed six-gill), up to 2.1m (7 ft) in length, prefers rather warmer waters than its larger relative, occurring around Florida, the Philippines, Madagascar, and the east African coast from Kenya to Natal.

Classification: *Mustelus canis* (family Triakidae); also known as the dusky smooth hound

Range: Western North Atlantic, from Cape Cod to Uruguay, and from southern Brazil to northern Argentina, including Cuba, Jamaica, Barbados, Bermuda and the Bahamas

Coloration: Dark grey or brownish, varying to a translucent pearly hue, changes in colour being accomplished by expansion or contraction of melanophores. The undersurfaces are whitish

Size: Up to 1.5m (5 ft) in length

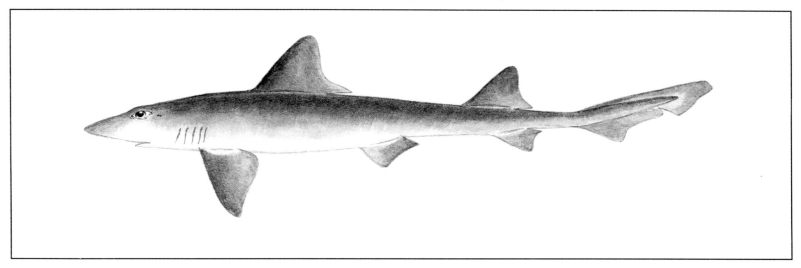

Description: Extremely common along the continental shelf of the western Atlantic, including the Caribbean, the smooth dogfish feeds principally on bottom-dwelling fish, crabs and lobsters, and is a typical member of this successful and abundant family, which occurs worldwide in enormous numbers. The snout of the smooth dogfish is not markedly elongate, while the teeth are small and rounded with slightly sinuous biting edges. There are two dorsal fins, the first of which is the larger, the second being situated immediately above the anal fin; the tail is relatively short, with only a small lower lobe. Reproduction is viviparous, with 10-20 pups each about 30cm (1 ft) in length at birth, constituting a litter; during development the embryos are attached to a nutritive placenta by means of a yolk sac and umbilical cord. The melanophore-generated colour change is a relatively slow process, transition to the palest coloration requiring as much as two days. The species appears to undertake seasonal migrations to warmer waters during the winter months, returning to higher latitudes in spring.

SPINY DOGFISH

Classification: *Squalus acanthias* (family Squalidae); also known as the piked dogfish or spur dog
Range: Temperate to sub-polar waters of the northern and southern hemispheres with a temperature range of 4.5–15.5°C (40–60°F). Greenland to Florida and the Canary Islands, the Mediterranean, the Black Sea, the Bering Strait to northern China and Baja California, southern Australia, New Zealand, Chile, South Africa
Coloration: Slate grey, sometimes tinged with brown, white spots
Size: Up to about 1m (3 ft 3 in) in length

Description: This common, small but voracious species occurs in shallow offshore water between the low water mark and the edge of the continental shelf, where it hunts fast-moving prey such as capelin, herring, menhaden, mackerel and haddock, as well as taking crustaceans (lobsters), worms, jellyfish, and even consuming red, brown and green algae. Sleekly proportioned with long graceful pectoral fins, no anal fin, and a broad tail incorporating a well developed lower lobe, the spiny dogfish owes its common name to the presence of a defensive spine in front of each of the two dorsal fins: up to a third of these spines is emergent from the flesh, and they each incorporate a poison gland at the base containing venom that will cause severe incapacitation in a human. Spiny dogfish undertake extensive seasonal migrations, moving polewards in summer and back towards lower latitudes in winter. Reproduction is ovo-viviparous, the gestation period being up to two years (longer than that of any other vertebrate animal), the 4-8 pups of each litter being 20–24cm (8–9½ in) in length at birth. Individual spiny dogfish may live for 30 years, to judge from the alternating light and dark growth rings found in the second dorsal spine.

SWELL SHARK

Classification: *Cephaloscyllium ventriosum* (family Scyliorhinidae).
Range: Coastal waters off California, southern Mexico and central Chile; its presence off western central America, Colombia and Ecuador has not been positively confirmed

Coloration: Brownish, with indistinct brown blotches and saddle marks
Size: About 1m (3 ft 3 in) in length

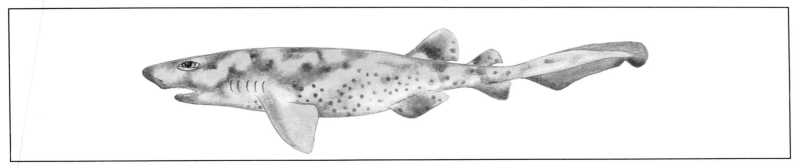

Description: These bottom-dwellers are slow, weak swimmers and usually feed at night, spending the daylight hours with their heads thrust into crevices. They are known as swell sharks because the stomach can be inflated with air or water as a defensive mechanism, the corners of the mouth being folded to accommodate the resulting stretching. When thus inflated these sharks are exceedingly difficult to remove from rocky underwater crevices, their small, spiny dermal denticles holding them firmly in place. The brown rectangular egg cases are secured by filaments to corals at a depth of about 50m (165 ft). New born individuals exhibit a row of enlarged denticles along the upper flanks and it has been surmised that these are to assist the embryo in escaping from its egg case: the hooked blades would provide a purchase on the ruptured edge of the case as the emergent juvenile wriggled to free itself. Half a dozen other species are recognized, occurring in the western Pacific, off southern Australia, in the northern Indian Ocean, off the south-east coast of Africa, and possibly in the Gulf of Aden.

THRESHER SHARK

Classification: *Alopias vulpinus* (family Alopiidae); also known as the fox shark, thrasher, whip-tailed shark, sickletail, swingletail and swiveltail
Range: Worldwide in temperate and subtropical waters, from Norway to South Africa, Newfoundland to Argentina, Japan to New Zealand, and British Columbia to Chile
Coloration: Dark greyish-brown to nearly black on the back and upper flanks, changing relatively abruptly to white ventrally; undersurfaces of pectoral fins leaden-hued
Size: Up to 6m (about 20 ft) in length, about half of which is contributed by the tail

Description: Distinguished by an extraordinarily elongate upper tail fin lobe, which is widely believed to function as a 'thresher' for driving schools of fish closer together so that they can more easily be caught. Authoritative eye witness accounts of such a practice are somewhat lacking, however, and the true purpose of the long tail is uncertain. A short snouted, blunt-nosed shark with small, flat triangular teeth, the thresher grows to a considerable size and is generally regarded as dangerous to man, although it does not seem to be a maneater; however, a gaffed specimen can cause serious injury to fishermen with its massive flailing tail when it is being hauled aboard a boat. The diet includes herring, shad, mackerel, and pilchards. Reproduction is ovo-viviparous, with 2–4 young (about 1.5m, nearly 5 ft, long) in a litter. A thresher with very large eyes (*Alopias superciliosus*) occurs in the western Atlantic and is possibly a deep-sea bottom-dweller, while several other species have been described from the Pacific.

Classification: *Galeocerdo cuvier* (family Carcharhinidae)

Range: Worldwide in tropical and subtropical seas, from Massachusetts to Uruguay, the British Isles to Angola, Indian Ocean coasts, Japan to New Zealand, southern California to Peru

Coloration: Nearly uniform greyish-brown; immature individuals are pale brown with dark brown bars and spots (hence the popular name)

Size: Up to 6m (about 20 ft) in length, with a weight of 1,350kg (about 3,000 lb)

Description: A powerfully proportioned and dangerous shark with large, flat, sickle-shaped teeth exhibiting coarsely serrated edges. The head is broad (almost square when viewed from above), with conspicuously large nostrils located near the end of the snout, and the upper lobe of the tail is unusually long for a member of the carcharhinid family.

Only a small second dorsal fin is present, immediately above the comparably reduced anal fin, but the first dorsal is tall and the pectoral fins well developed. This shark has been responsible for a long catalogue of attacks on people and is so voracious that when hungry it will swallow almost anything it encounters; the stomachs of dead tiger sharks have been found to contain such innutritious items as pieces of coal, cushions from boats, tin cans, cigarette packets, plastic bags, and even, on one occasion, a tom-tom. Their normal diet comprises other sharks, all kinds of fish (even stingrays), porpoises, turtles, sea birds, sea lions, squid, octopus, crabs, molluscs, crabs and lobsters. Reproduction is ovo-viviparous, with 10 to over 80 small embryos measuring only 0.5m (1 ft 6 in) in a litter. Relatively little is known about the life habits of tiger sharks, and they rarely survive long in captivity.

TOPE

Classification: *Galeorhinus galeus* (family Carcharhinidae); also known as the toper, white hound or penny dog
Range: Temperate waters of the eastern Atlantic (Iceland to South Africa), western Atlantic (southern Brazil to Argentina), Mediterranean, and the Pacific (Australia, New Zealand, British Columbia to the Gulf of California, Peru to Chile)
Coloration: Brownish or dusky grey above, paler below; the front of both dorsal fins and the tip of the caudal are black
Size: Up to 2m (6 ft 6 in) in length

Description: A cosmopolitan bottom-dwelling species that in the eastern Atlantic occurs as far north as Iceland and as far south as South Africa, with a north-south Pacific range extending from British Columbia to New Zealand. It is not present in the western North Atlantic, an absence that is difficult to explain. Fierce and voracious despite their moderate size, topes feed mostly on small fish, crustaceans, starfish and shellfish, as well as scavenging, typically occurring at depths of 40–400m (130–1,300 ft). The teeth, set obliquely in the jaws, are notched and exhibit serrate edges; the eye is proportionately large, the dorsal fin tall, and the tail rather short. Reproduction is viviparous, with up to about 50 pups born to each pregnant female in the summer months, usually in shallow water (e.g. in enclosed bays and estuaries). Tope occur in small schools, and migrate polewards in summer, equatorially in winter, sometimes covering nearly 60km (almost 40 miles) a day for distances of 1,600km (1,000 miles).

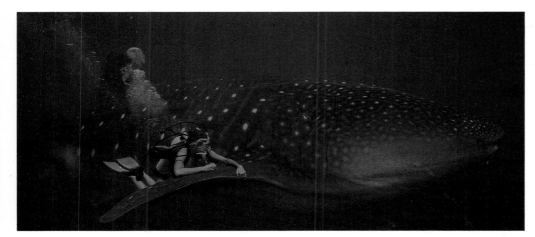

WHALE SHARK

Classification: *Rhincodon typus* (family Rhincodontidae)
Range: Tropical Atlantic (New York to Brazil, Senegal to the Gulf of Guinea), Pacific (Japan to northern Australia, southern California to Chile) and Indian Oceans
Coloration: Grey or brownish, paler ventrally, with round white or yellow spots, closely spaced on the head but separated by narrow vertical streaks of the same colour on the body
Size: Up to 15m (50 ft) in length, weighing up to 20 tonnes

Description: The largest living fish, but harmless to man, subsisting on anchovies, sardines, small albacores, tuna and squid, with plankton strained from the water by a system of cartilaginous bars covered in spongy tissue that connect the gill openings internally and act in conjunction with prominent, denticle-covered papillae lining the oesophagus to form a highly efficient sieve. The body is flattened anteriorly, with a broad head and short, very wide mouth. There are two dorsal fins (the front one up to 1.2m, 4 ft, tall), the upper lobe of the tail fin is much longer than the lower lobe, and two or three lateral keels run along each side of the body, with a single median ridge. Whale sharks are said frequently to feed while nearly vertical in the water, and rely less exclusively on filter feeding than the basking shark, whose very large gill slits, huge mouth and expandable throat can accommodate a much greater throughput of water. The teeth of whale sharks are small and curved, forming a rasp-like dentition. No definite conclusions concerning the reproductive process have been reached, although an egg 30cm (12 in) long containing an unmistakable whale shark embryo measuring 35cm (13¾ in) was trawled up in 1953, and a pregnant female caught subsequently contained a number of egg capsules.

ZEBRA SHARK

Classification: *Stegostoma fasciatum* (family Orectolobidae); also known as the leopard shark or tiger shark (not to be confused with the true tiger shark, *Galeocerdo cuvier*)

Range: Red Sea, Indian Ocean, western Pacific from Australasia north to Japan

Coloration: Yellowish-white with dark brown spots, the pattern varying between individuals. Young zebra sharks exhibit a saddle-stripe marking (hence the popular name) which eventually breaks up to form a characteristic spotted pattern

Size: Up to about 4m (13 ft) in length

Description: A tropical bottom-dweller mostly active at night, the zebra shark is a strikingly marked species of considerable size, although the unusually long tail (with no lower lobe) can represent nearly half of the total overall measurement. Its head is broad and somewhat flattened with a rounded snout and short, pointed sensory barbels adjacent to the nostrils. The spiracle is very large, almost equalling the eye in size, and the front edge of the first dorsal fin arises from the back in front of the level at which the pelvic fins are joined to the lower flanks. There is a series of prominent longitudinal ridges running along the body, and the tail angles upwards at only a slight angle. Zebra sharks are common on coral reefs, their slender, flexible bodies enabling them to enter narrow crevices in search of the molluscs, crabs, shrimps and small bony fish on which they feed. Reproduction is oviparous, with up to four eggs in each oviduct; after laying, the dark brown horny egg capsules are attached to the substrate by means of long, barb-like filaments. The skin of the zebra shark produces an excellent shagreen.

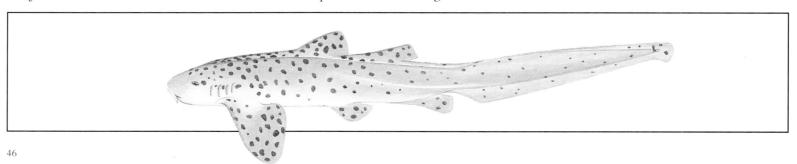